Promises

THE POETRY OF THE ZADOKIM

Cassondra E. Beers

Eyedentified Publishing Solutions, SPRINGDALE, ARKANSAS

Library of Congress Control Number: 2016944965

Eyedentified Consulting Services, LLC
d/b/a Eyedentified Publishing Solutions
P.O. Box 6892
Springdale, AR 72766-6892
www.eyedentifiedconsulting.com

Publisher's Note: This is a work of fiction. Names, characters, places, and incidents are a product of the author's imagination. Locales and public names are sometimes used for atmospheric purposes. Any resemblance to actual people, living or dead, or to businesses, companies, events, institutions, or locales is completely coincidental. Any expletive language used is the express position of the author and not an endorsement express or implied by Eyedentified Consulting Services, LLC or its affiliates.

Book Layout © 2015 BookDesignTemplates.com

Publisher's Cataloging-In-Publication Data
(Prepared by The Donohue Group, Inc.)

Names: Beers, Cassondra E.
Title: Promises : the poetry of the Zadokim / Cassondra E. Beers.
Description: 1st ed. | Springdale, Arkansas : Eyedentified Publishing
     Solutions, [2016]
Identifiers: LCCN 2016944965 | ISBN 978-1-945566-00-4 (hardcover) | ISBN
     978-0-9966649-9-8 (trade paper) | ISBN 978-1-945566-01-1 (Kindle) |
     978-1-945566-02-8 (ebook)
Subjects: LCSH: God (Christianity)--Faithfulness--Poetry. | Righteousness
     --Poetry. | Christian poetry.
Classification: LCC PS3602.E47 P76 2016 (print) | LCC PS3602.E47 (ebook) |
     DDC 811/.6--dc23mpletely coincidental.

I would like to thank all of the Zadokim who have taken their places and helped me find mine.

CONTENTS

What is a Zadokim?

In 2012, I began to know myself as I drew closer to Yahweh. As a result of this, He gave me a word: Zadokim. I took the name Zadok, which means righteousness in Hebrew, and the suffix –im and put them together. This was meant to mean "sons of righteousness" and call out a group of people who choose to be sons of Yahweh and allow Him to lead them in the paths of righteousness. I later learned that the suffix –im is used to denote plurality in the Hebrew language. Thus, the nuance of "righteous ones" was added to the meaning "sons of righteousness."

I discovered that I had—through my relationship with Holy Spirit—actually created a word that already existed in a deviated form: the Hebrew word tzadikkim, which is the root word of "Sadducees."

I did not want any association with the Sadducees as described in the Bible, but Yahweh is a redeemer and He did not create the word Zadokim to be used by the Sadducees in the way that it was. He told me to reclaim that word for His glory.

It is a great honor to have Yahweh choose you as one who will redeem a word. It is also quite funny to me that He did so by allowing me to think I had made the word up when it existed in an ancient language that I do not actually speak.

But what does it mean to be a Zadokim? Yahweh has shown me—and continues to show me—through scripture, revelation, and poetry. We are the ones who choose to minister to Yahweh, to offer Him our lives and everything else. We are the ones to whom He reveals His heart and mind, the ones He then allows to carry His heart and mind into all creation, showing creation His original intentions even as we embrace his original intentions for ourselves.

It is my hope that this word sparks a Holy Spirit inspired revelation in you of your unique promise and importance in the kingdom of Yahweh. I declare that each of you begin the journey to become Zadokim and are reconciled back to whom you were originally created to be before time began. We are on this journey together.

Thanks for reading!

Cassondra E. Beers

Part I: Promises

The Promise

Wherever you go I shall find you

And wherever you are, there I'll be

And I shall always remind you

Of your identity.

I have not left you to perish

You shall not wither or die

You are my son whom I cherish

My witness to testify.

I place you in this earthen vessel

That which you claim and restore

Then you come again to the rest

And claim your unvarnished reward.

Together we walk in creation

As one, united, hand in hand

Redeeming each tribe, tongue, and nation

Uniting the beasts, herbs, and land.

And now it's back to the beginning

The place where it also shall end

You are my promised redemption

That which before me I send.

The Promises I Keep

Into the world my mind is thrown

Beyond all reaches that I've known

I cannot fathom the depths below

As my experiences show

The miles stretch out in endless array

Before me now, a brand new day

I cannot think, I cannot say

Sometimes I even forget the way

Yet the Way leads forward, onward

And I will stand atop the strong Word

Provision, purpose, on the long road

Guide me gently, tear down strongholds

A greater truth is kept in promises

Given, made, and unabandoned

I receive, yet I must keep

The promises made unto me

With my troth I pledge me willing

To keep the promise to me entrusted

And through interminable nature, thrilling

I shall rise and stand above this

In quiet trust I stand now, waiting

Though my heart is sorely aching

The hope I have, steady unshaken

That I have never been forsaken

The promise spoken in the Word

The Promise I have seen and heard

My aching heart is again stirred

And I keep going undeterred

Draw me up, in courage arm me

Thousands shall fall, but it won't hit me

I won't die, no I shall live free

Promise now, oh Yahweh, help me

Holding tightly to the Promise

Made and kept to and from Oneness

I shall never leave you homeless

Steady on now, keep the Promise.

Righteousness

A covenant, a Promise

Made before time directly to you

Directly from Yahweh

And received by faith.

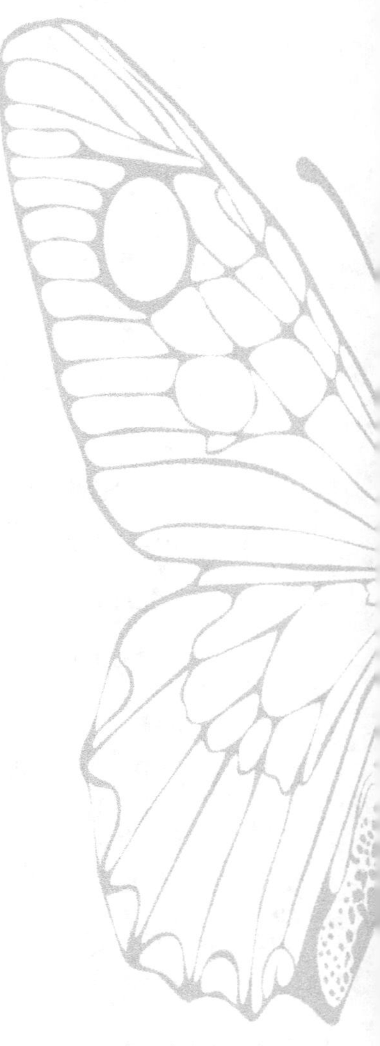

Part I: Promises

Home

Lights shine from the windows of an empty house

And this is more than I had before

But there is more that I'm waiting for

A home Yahweh has for me in store

Home is where a Father is

Protecting and loving all His kids

Reigning over those who are His

Keeping safe and inviting in

Home is where the Father loves

Where He says, "You are enough."

Where you are secure in enormous hugs

Sheltered and covered around and above

Something I've never had before

And oh how my heart has longed for more

Yet when I enter my front door

A dog awaits and nothing more

Where is my Father, my home to be?

Where can I rest and learn to see?

Where can I feel safe, secure, and free?

Why is no home reserved for me?

But Yahweh has greater than I've ever known

He waited to give me a home that's His own

More glorious than houses or palatial thrones

Yahweh made me His son and through me He shone

For what I don't have is nothing I have lost

For Yahweh sat down and He counted the cost

Gave His own Son so that I could be bought

Securing my place in the lineage He wrought

For I have a Father and this is my home

Secure in His arms, a son all His own

And when I feel lonely, I just have to know

My Father is love and I'm never alone.

Peace

Oh! What a marvelous thing
To be at peace with your God
And yourself.

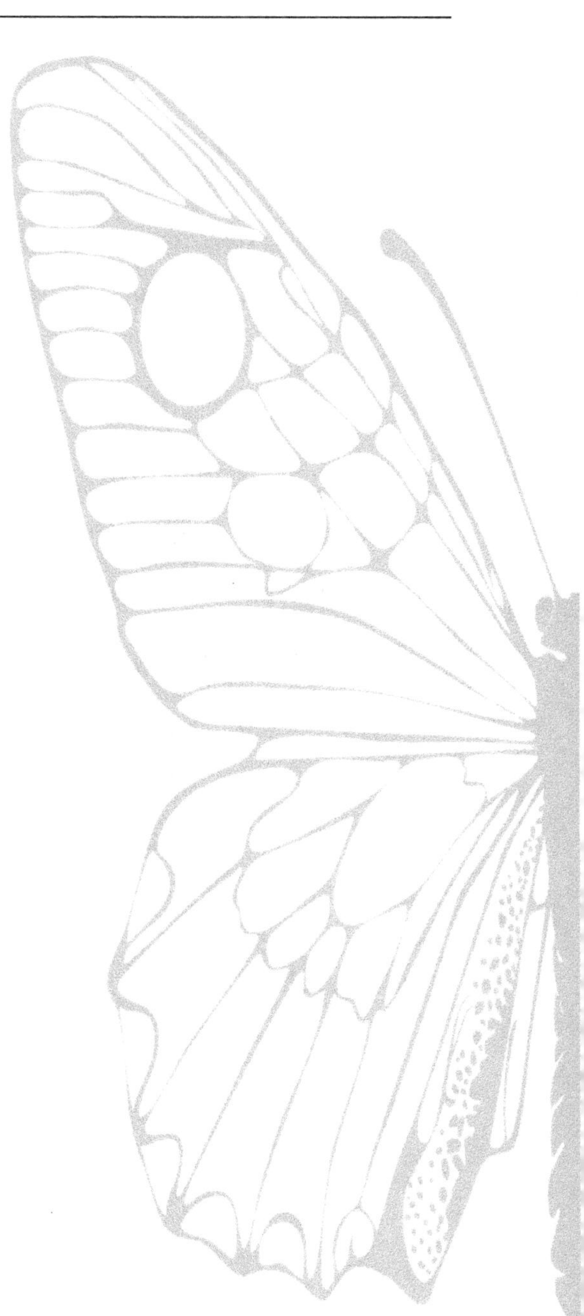

Wisdom

Eyes to see what I've always seen

Mind to know what I already know

Heart to sing what I will always sing

Able to go where I've already gone.

Ears to hear words spoken

That resonate throughout time

Faith to fix what was never broken

And claim what has always been mine.

For it is life to us who are already living

For we have always been alive

Always receiving the promise we're giving

As we are One with Christ.

Part I: Promises

Stability

Safety, peace, a place of rest

Purpose in the Father

A certainty that I am blessed,

Provided for, and authored.

A lack of changeability

Immutable as Truth

Unshakeable, the Rock of Grace

Yahweh's promised oath.

Abiding in the Father,

There within to dwell

Growing in wisdom and stature

From foundation's wealth.

A peace that I have never known

A place to work and play

Yahweh's given me a home

To live, love, and create.

Joy

Oh! The joy

Of being with my Father

Abiding in His Presence

Just soaking Him in!

Part I: Promises

Perfect Love Casts Out Fear

If perfect love does cast out fear

Then Lord, what are we doing here?

How does this fit into your plan?

Except that I can take a stand.

It's time to show fear who is boss

To stand and win against the loss

It's such an opportunity

To give Yahweh His great glory.

If only I abide in love,

I needn't fight; that is enough

There, perfection I will find

The very foundation of my life.

Deep in the heart of my Father

I will go and find myself

I will not seek another

In His New Covenant I will dwell.

Trusting my Father to bring me

All that I ever will need

Allowing Him to redeem me

Letting Him set me free.

Thank You, Yahweh, oh thank You

For the Covenant that's new

For fixing all that was broken

By bringing it into You.

Just as easily flowing

As the River that brings life

You've given my heart a knowing

That I don't have to strive.

All I have I remember

As you bring it back to mind

The Promise returning to sender

But never doing so void.

Faithfully I wait in Your Presence

Faithfully, You fill me whole

All that I have I surrender

And receive back a hundredfold.

Worship

We enter the presence of Yahweh

And everything else comes to order

Nothing matters but Him

And we become who we really are.

Success

I cannot help but be

Who Yahweh's called me

For this is Yahweh's Promise

He's the Promise Keeper

The Promised Words of Life

That He spoke before time

Into my ear now

Faithfully, He whispers:

Whatever happens to you

When I send you out

I will come and find you

To empower

I will work through you

I will give you clout

I've made a promise

Nothing can undo you

You have to be successful

There is no other way

I've woven success

Into your very nature

I will be right beside you

I'm with you every day

Whispering the promise

I made to you

Go out and walk in victory

Your victory assured

The enemy has truly

Nothing on you

For I will keep my Promise

You are my Promised Word

I've changed the course of history

To own you.

Myself

Once,

Yahweh gave me life, gave me myself

Then He waited to see if I would give me back to Him.

I did.

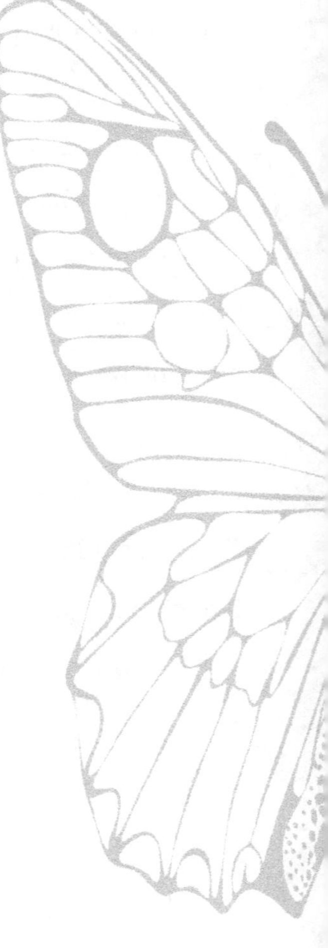

Part I: Promises

Lake of Revelation

Dip a toe into the lake of Yahweh's revelation

But when you do, prepare yourself for the tidal wave to come

For Yahweh longs to speak to us, to share His great elation

The joy He has imbues us all with Yahweh's great wisdom

Sow to the Spirit and not to the flesh, just spend time with the Father

He will give you all that is left, adding one thing on another

There is no need to seek it out, just trust and it will come,

For Yahweh made us to abide in His house, to receive His perfect love

Take the hand that is stretched out and learn the ways of Heaven

Do not allow yourself to doubt that Yahweh's Word is true

For if you learn what Yahweh knows, you will not be a child

In leaving all your childish ways, you become more like you

Such great perspective you will have with Yahweh's revelation

The Truth of Heaven you can bring and walk in on the Earth

Only through faith and hope will you know this jubilation

For we can only receive in faith what Yahweh wants us to learn

So dip a toe into the lake of Yahweh's revelation

He will give you all good things, just wait for them to come

For Yahweh's joy is to speak with us, to all the tribes and nations

To make us all into what He saw, His righteous, faithful sons.

Life

A Father goes out

To find His lost sons

And then teaches them His way.

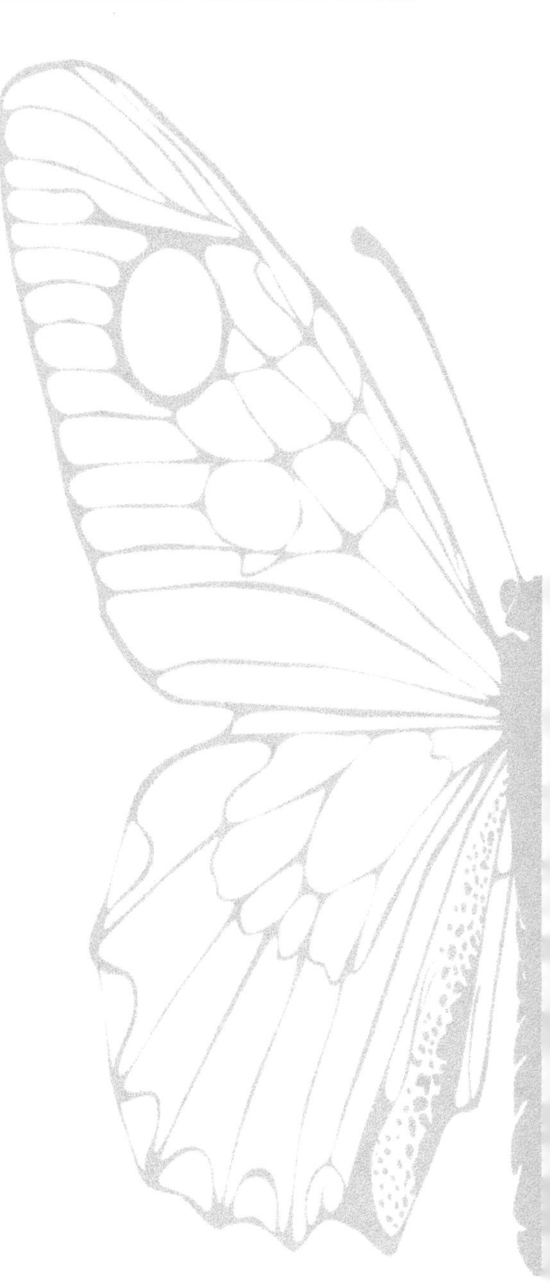

Vision

The greatest story ever told, a canvas painted bright

A symphony with sounds of old, a tapestry of delight

The bigger picture, puzzle's frame, perspective's greatest gift

Yahweh's big purpose, vision's faith, a view of all there is.

A thread inside the tapestry, a note in symphonic sound

A brushstroke in a painted scene, a seed under the ground

A single line of poetry, a simple human heart

How can we see all that's come to be when we are just a part?

Sometimes we give obedience for what we don't understand

Sometimes Yahweh gives us a gift and shows us some of His plan

Sometimes we see and know in part, how can we know in full?

For what's inside the Father's Heart's much bigger than all we've known.

The vision's greater than the part, for truly there's a whole

The glory of my Father is He's given us His all

Inside the vision He has placed a vision for us to see

Amazingly a single thread holds the entire tapestry.

Christ in you is glory's hope, and glory shall be found

When symphony's individual notes choose to lay themselves down

Part submitting to the whole, it's greater than just me!

And when I say "I do not know," I can begin to see.

I am a part of something great, a word inside a poem

A word that shall not return void, for I am Yahweh's own

And He has made a place for me; He doesn't make mistakes

A vision of a tapestry, creation for Yahweh's sake.

Give up what seemed important once, and though you may be saddened

Seek ye first the Kingdom of God and all else will be added

For if you try to care for parts, you'll never see the vision

But if the Big Picture's in your heart, the rest shall have provision.

In diligently seeking Yahweh's face, I can see with His eyes

And all He purposed when He created in fullness shall arise

Pressing onward, ever upward, toward the higher call

I'll know when I embrace the vision I've given it my all.

Willingly I lay down my life to give Yahweh the glory

But isn't that what Yahshua did for the joy that comes in the morning?

He saw the vision, Yahweh's plan, He reckoned up the cost

Then He became a mortal man and hung upon a cross.

We let go of what was, what we thought to be, we let go of limited sight

We give up on ourselves and become free, letting Yahweh have our lives

We know in the end, He's the only One who can ever make us perfect

And it's His vision, in Him we trust, for we know that He is worth it.

Such joyous glory set before, a vision for all to see

When single notes become a chorus and threads become tapestry

And I shall stand and take my part, in vision here to dwell

For I shall have my Father's heart and His mind as well.

And when I see the fullness of Yahweh my God and Father

I shall forever sing His praise and worship like no other

Though many elders 'round His throne sing "Holy, holy, holy"

I worship Him in ways my own as I give Him all the glory.

For each part needs to take its place in Bigger Picture's vision

Here Yahweh's given us a way to be creative with Him

We may choose to fulfill our role, our purpose manifesting

Then, though parts, we become whole, while in our Father resting.

For though I see now but in part, I am still fully known

One day I'll see all my Father's heart and in fullness make my home

All time and space will then collapse, the veil be fully lifted

And I shall sit on my Father's lap in the completed vision.

Family

When Yahshua the Son

Takes His Bride home

To meet His Father.

Beauty

Zoom out and see the tapestry

The whole picture of creation

Examine all and you will see

My coming jubilation

The joy is set before you

Only if you live in time

For the joy is now within you

If you just see with My eyes

So expand your field of vision

See My glorious revelation

Abide in joy that you were given

Enhance your expectation

Flaws and imperfections

Cease to be when brought to light

For in the beauty of redemption

I have made everything right

So take your place in the tapestry

Lift up your head and bow your knee

Be who you've always been to Me

The beauty of My majesty

This joy with which I strengthen thee

I have come and set you free

To be the beauty that I see

Complete and holy, graced, redeemed

All I've created, I do see

My joy is now fully complete

And if you will abide in Me

You will receive the promised peace

The beauty of My ornament

The glory set within

A tapestry of adornments

And all there truly is

Oh the beauty of the whole picture

Can be seen in each component

If you by faith and with stature

Stand up and truly own it

So take your place in My tapestry

Lift up your head and bow your knee

See who you are, you'll always be

The glory of my tapestry

My redemption, beauty, whole, complete.

Perfection

Oh! The utter, exquisite beauty

Of Perfection

Experienced in worship

As we enter the Presence

Of Yahweh whom we love.

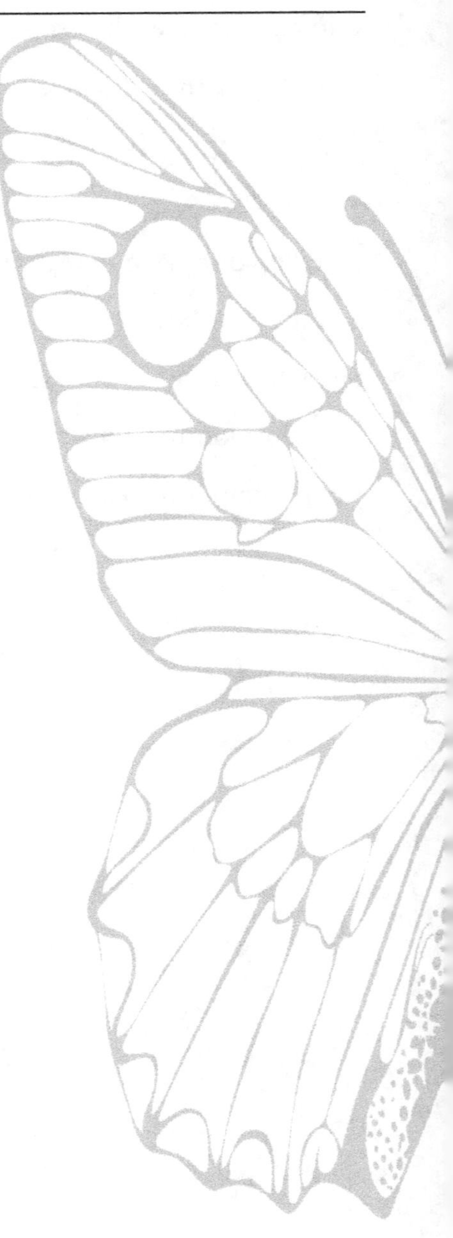

Part I: Promises

Wholeness

More than fixing what is broken

More than deliverance and health,

But taking all that ever was

And making it His story tell

For every thread in a tapestry

And every line in a poem

Has purpose beyond what it can see

As it fits inside the whole

The times I thought that I would die

Give great meaning to my life

And all the times I tried and tried

Make me glad for rest from strife

The things I used to never have

But now live in each day

Give rise to praises unimagined

And remind me I am safe

And what in me was grown through times

I felt so lost and broken

But wisdom, grace, a joy for life

And faith in the Word that was spoken

A single thread in a tapestry

Can't be judged on a small part that's woven

And a life that a pure-hearted human leads

Cannot rightly be judged on a moment

Amazing grace, how can it be

How awesome is Yahweh who's spoken

That He can come and all redeem

Bring wholeness from all that was broken.

Faith

Agreeing

That the Word, the Promise, the Covenant

That Yahweh spoke into being

Before time ever existed

Still is.

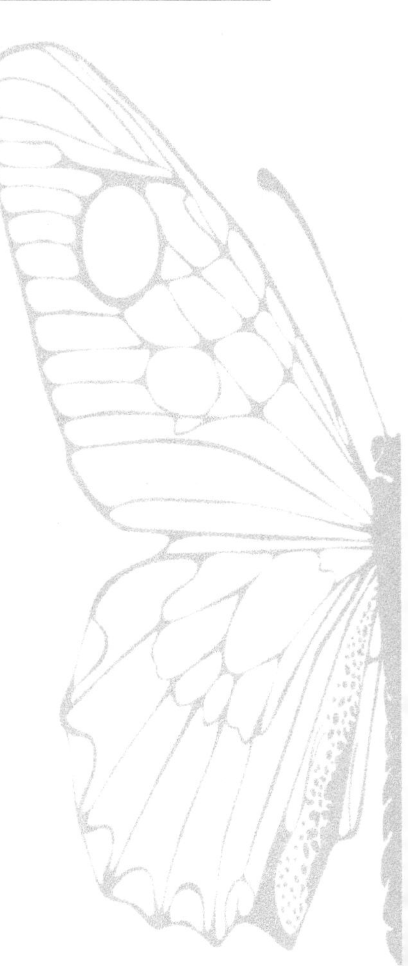

Remembering

I have made a Way for you

To come into a place

A place where you remember who

I made you now in grace

Remembering the Promises

I spoke into your being

Remembering the love I give

Remembering the dreams

I have made a Way for you

To remember who you are

To operate in faith and truth

To be light in the dark

The Words I whispered in your heart

When I spoke to frame the worlds

The Word you heard and can impart

More value than many pearls

When I spoke to create you

I had such great delight

I was so joyful to make you

For I hid treasures deep inside

Remember now what I said

When I spoke you into being

Your essence is My Promises

The Promises I keep

I could not stand to lose you

Thought it cost Me everything

I kept the promised pattern

Of the tapestry of being

I promised to restore you

And to bring you back to life

The life I gave you to express

The heart I had inside

The hope of all the Promises

The glory of My Christ

The faithfulness by which you live

The light you stand to shine

Remember all My Promises

And tell them to the world

Remind creation it should live

To be my priceless pearl.

Rest

To know You were done

Before You started

Creation was won

Before You started

And we were Your sons

Before You started

Yahweh, by You I was loved

Before You started.

A Place

I go prepare a place for you,

I will come back again

I stay to prepare you for the place

That's your Beginning and your End

The place that I created,

The vision I expressed

Such beauty in perfection

All majesty, all rest

Then I created you in My endless love

I authored you in that place

Where only goodness and light abide

Only righteousness and grace

I wanted you for a reason,

I made you the perfect shape

To pour a facet of Myself,

A part of what I did create

I have made a place for you

Because I made you for a place

That place in Me, your home, your truth
You return to it by faith!

Stand up and take your rightful place
I made you there to dwell
I sent My Son to bring you back
From the very gates of Hell

I created you in a moment, a place
Where time and space were one
In infinite-eternity, you I did shape
Then sent you to the Earth as sons

I called you back from the abyss
Perfected, I made you whole
I've drawn you up into righteousness
Complete in body, spirit, and soul

Now looking at you, I have such delight
Oh what I did create!
I called it good, I called it right
At the end of every day

I made you to be a light

The darkness cannot comprehend you

Here in the place where you abide

Exactly where I had planned you

Ascribe to the upward call, come to new heights

But you've been here before

For this was your home ere you were alive

All I've done is reopen the door

You were meant to be here, you were meant to be loved,

You were meant to abide in truth

You were meant to be perfect and you are enough

No matter what you happen to do

A place in the vision, a vision of grace

I've given you now a home

But only because you I did create

To be in this place with Me, whole

So take your place in the vision,

Allow the vision to take place in you

For this reason, I have arisen

For this I created you.

Reconciliation

Oh, how amazing

That there is One

Who can reconcile two opposing things

Whole and part,

Justice and mercy,

Love and righteousness,

That He can take what was broken and make it whole,

That by fixing it, redeeming it,

He can make new things out of broken things,

Beauty from ashes

Joy and mourning.

All things together and goodness.

Oh the majesty, the tapestry, the beauty of redemption,

Of reconciling dichotomies

Only Yahweh

Only, only Yahweh.

Existence

We exist!

And we shall never, ever be lost.

Yahweh will seek us, and He will find us,

And He will offer us a way back to Himself.

Confirmation's Oath

Once again you ask that I let go of the past

But that's so hard when past is still the present

Once again I choose seemingly to lose

Knowing that in You all things are given

Though You've promised to bless me, still it can be so hard

To give up what I've worked for, longed to keep

Though it seems overwhelming, I will let go and move on

But not for what You said You'd give to me

I will be like Abraham sacrificing Isaac

For I will have such rich, abiding faith

I will be like Yahshua laying down His life

And I will do it all just for Your sake

For You are what I've truly wanted, yearned for all along

The blessings and the joys are incidental

Though it hurts to give them up, for You I will move on

You're the joy that's set before me, my dear Treasure

So I will rise up and ascend to the places where You are

I will go and be what You have called me

I will faithfully abide in the Covenant of Love

And choose the bread and wine that You are offering

I will be like Gideon, leading his three hundred

For I don't need a sword to save the day

I will be a king and priest of all that You have spoken

Because I seek You only, oh Yahweh

Of whom much is given much also is required

For You must test all such worthy hearts

To know that You alone, Yahweh, are all that we desire

Sometimes You call us to let all else depart

So I will be like Abraham sacrificing Isaac

Like You were when You gave the world to man

Knowing when You did so that we would be separated

But You would come and save us once again

For redemption wins forever when all is said and done

But nothing can ever be truly lost

If we can lay down our lives and all that we have won

For vision's sake, count worthy all the cost

If sacrifice of all, Yahweh, is all that it will take

Well, we do no less than Yahshua, our elder Brother

We do no less than You did when You chose to create

Then placed creation in the hands of another

You gave away all that You had willingly on that day

To see if it was ever truly Yours

Then, Yahweh, You brought it back, for it is Yours always

Confirmation's Oath makes Promises assured

An Oath of Confirmation brings an end to all dispute

So I receive the Promise of the Father

By giving away everything when He calls me to choose

And getting to return home to my Father.

Memory

Oh! What a marvelous thing

To remember the Promise,

To remember the Word that was spoken to me

When I became a living being.

Vision Carriers

We are the vision carriers

We are the fountains of dreams

We can express Yahweh's Kingdom

But first we must learn how to see

He placed His vision inside us

His glory, Christ's hope, to express

And once we see it in ourselves

We can show the world Yahweh's best

We carry on Yahweh's vision

As we allow Him to strip us bare

That all can be seen for His glory

His vision exposed to be shared

We were made just for this purpose

That Yahweh's perfection arise

It's not about doing or works

It's about seeing our own facet of Christ

Christ inside me is the hope of glory

As I take Him wherever I go

I weave the tapestry's pattern

As I allow Him to lead me home

When from Him I went, He did find me

Wherever I am, there He is

And He did come back and remind me

That I have always been His

Then He gently removed every layer

Of lies in which I learned to hide

He heard my heart's deep cry and prayer

He redeemed me from the inside

The light inside's now burning brightly

That it can be seen from without

Expressing the vision of my Father

Alleviating creation's doubts

In receiving the promise of my Father

I am able to promise as well

Shining the light before others

So that they can see Him in themselves

Wherever I go, Yahweh's in me

He abides here forever to show

Simply by allowing Him to redeem me

I've made His vision known.

Part II:
The New Covenant

The Law of Love

Once beyond all time in a Kingdom outside space

There lived a Father God who was longing to create

So He took a bit of passion and He spoke the Word aloud

So the beauty deep within His mind could be seen without.

Once upon a time, He created time and space

And filled it with His wonder, His glory, and His grace

Delighting in all that He made, He declared it to be good

He set the laws of time and space so things would be as they
should.

Once upon a time, He created a being called man

To him He gave such power as the steward of the land

In this the man was truly blessed, for walking with His God

He could carry out his Father's behest and return to Him His
love.

Once upon a time, it was given to man to choose,

For love can't ever be coerced if it's ever to be true

And man walked with his Father in the cool of the day

Whatever Word his Father spoke, the man sought to obey.

Once upon a darkened time, the man did choose awry

And all creation trembled in unutterable cry

But the Father God did have a plan, for this was no surprise;

He holds creation in His hand and sees with Heaven's eyes.

His love did supersede all time, did overcome all space

The law of love did triumph over all He did create

So taking a new form, the Father stepped down to the Earth

Fulfilling all His promises, taking upon Himself the curse.

So with this act of sacrifice, the Father did redeem

What man had thrown into the fire, what was dirty He has cleaned

He fixed the broken tapestry, He mended what was torn

He resurrected passion's glee, from night He made the morn.

The joy was set before Him and He gladly paid the price

So the beauty of His ornaments was again given to life

And man again was steward, a faithful righteous son

The law of love did give him breath to submit again to the One

Who made him in His inmost heart, who called him into being

Then gave to him a brand new start, forgiving him all things

He allowed man again to walk with Him, He allowed him to create

The ingredients in creation: Love, Word, Spirit, and Faith.

Now we can walk with our God, together we can dwell

With Him we can create in this world, in our minds create ourselves

Without Him, we are nothing; all we can do is receive

For if we want to be redeemed, we must have faith to believe.

In the law of love, I do believe, to Yahweh I submit

Triumphs, trials, circumstance, all else I do forfeit

For greater is the Prize indeed on which I set my eyes

Than anything I could receive from Babylonian lies.

And once upon a time in a Kingdom here today

I dwell in peace with Yahweh God, I live for Him always

Hearing and obeying, seeing life before my eyes

Such glory and such splendor that comes with knowing Christ.

Threads

Once there was a tapestry, woven of time and space

A Master Weaver, He did weave, knowing just what to create

A picture inside of His mind's eye, He set out to portray

Then taking space and time in hand, He created night and day.

He created planets, suns, and stars; He created minutes and hours

He created Earth, oceans, and skies; He did all this with His power

Out of His being came all that is, all that was or ever will be

Then He created human beings; He created you and me.

He created and He shared with us His glorious tapestry

Woven out of His pure love, He created perfectly

Each intersection of space and time, each thread in perfect line

His order, creation's laws, were set; all was truly divine.

The tapestry was perfect, of this there is no doubt

For if one thread was out of line, the whole thing would be out

Each and every intersection of each and every thread

Was exactly where it needed to be, not one broken or frayed.

Until the thing they call "the Fall" when man did choose awry

In breaking his thread, he broke them all; all of creation cried

The laws of space and time were broken, perfection truly lost

If only man had seen the threads and been able to count the cost!

For one thread broken, the tapestry fell, threads tangled in a knot

Some were frayed or snapped or torn; surely all was lost!

But the Master Weaver did not despair as He saw His tapestry

He had the power to repair, the power to redeem.

He could've thrown the tapestry out, could've started all again

But He has never thrown anything away just because it was broken

There was a law above all laws, all laws of space and time

The law of love allowed Him now to hear creation's cry.

He entered His own tapestry; the fibers He did bind

Each and every thread He did redeem, He gave to them new life

For if the laws of time and space dictate where the threads should fall

The law of love holds fibers in place so the threads are threads at all.

So entering His tapestry, He makes the threads themselves

By leaving in each of them a peace of the Master Weaver's self

Then the threads can once again in time and space exist

Make the beauty of the tapestry to the Master Weaver's bliss.

The Master Weaver is so pleased with the tapestry He wove

The tapestry, full and complete, when He started, it was done

It was in His mind, the law of love, ere the laws of time and space

It was this law, the law of love, that impelled Him to create.

So what was the Beginning is now the End; "It is finished!" He cried aloud

The Alpha and Omega of creation, He has spoken, so hear His sound

For those who have the ears to hear will know and understand

And praise the Master Weaver for His great and glorious plan.

Letting Go

Right! Wrong! Do this, don't do that!

Your life can turn upon a dime or at the drop of a hat!

Stop! Go! You have so much to do!

You can't just rest, cannot be still, you've got to muddle through!

If you don't, you will be WRONG, you will be WRONG I say!

And if you do not get it right, you'll never find your way

You won't be able to have joy, won't please your Father's heart

Instead, you'll languish unemployed, have nothing to impart.

Do! Don't! This law is very harsh!

If you fall and can't keep up, you're cast out in the dark!

Success! Failure! It's all just up to you

Listen now and hear me well, there's nothing you can do!

No wonder life is full of fear, who can live up to this?

But I think one time I did hear it's okay to take a risk

Right, wrong, forget it, there's no way!

Yahshua came and shed His blood so I could walk in grace.

Faith! Hope! The love of my Father's Truth

My Brother did fulfill the law, set me free to be, not do

Since He already shed His blood, He already made me right

So I won't worry about being wrong; He's already won the fight.

Rest! Peace! All comfort He bestows

I take it into my heart now, of right and wrong I do let go!

Come! Be! He calls the weary and faint of heart

I will give you lasting peace, remind you who you are!

Praise the Lord! He set me free to life

He took upon Himself the yoke and gave my eyes new sight

See! Know! Be yourself whom He called

Give glory to the one true King who is beyond all right and wrong.

Beyond All Right and Wrong

There is such freedom in the place

Beyond all right and wrong

Where Yahweh's called us to His faith

And given us His all

We focus on the Father's heart

And what He wants to say

Leaving behind all that we are

And choosing His paths and ways

We lean not on our own righteousness

But accepting His by faith,

We receive all that He says there is

We glorify Him always

Growing in authority

We become mature sons

Walking as Yahshua did

Doing only what the Father does

For when we eschew all right and wrong

We can see what the Father does teach us

For the Father loves His sons and shows us

All that we have need of.

Covenant of Love

My life was changed forever

When I learned what I always knew

When the law became a promise

Instead of things I have to do

Gone are the days of anger,

Guilt and frustration

Now I can walk in peace

In the Covenant of Love

My world was rocked again,

But I am used to that by now

I'm left with a foundation

That is just right somehow

For He knows just how to shake me

In a way that makes things right

It hurts, but doesn't break me

It sets me free to life

The foundation and assurance

Of the Covenant of Love

Yahweh's promise has endurance

It will always be enough

No matter what the shaking,

What the trials or the pain

The Promise of the Father

Will eternally remain

So come what may, oh Father

I will worship You and praise

For you didn't choose another

You have given me your grace

And the Covenant, the Promise

Of the life I live in You,

You are worth it if I'm honest

You're my inheritance, my truth

Should I go through the process

That shall give me more of You?

Oh the cost cannot be counted

I can't afford not to!

Gratitude

My heart overflows

With gratitude for everything

So much that even I can't show

In written words upon a page.

Oh, Father, You know!

Read my heart and see my life,

It's the best way I can show

The gratitude that's deep inside.

Can You imagine now

Just what my life would've been

If You had not come down

And rescued me from all those things?

I can imagine, see,

I used to live in misery

But now You've set me free

Given me visions, truth, and peace.

Yahshua, my Melchizedek,

Mediator of promises,

Without You I would be a wreck

I was so lost in deep sadness.

But You obeyed the Father,

Lived and died and rose again

Became High Priest forever

And to the Father access gave.

You truly are the Way,

The only Way back to my home

The Truth, the Life, all things

You've given me to be Your Own.

Without You I am nothing,

I would be dead outside and in

Instead, You've made my heart sing

Now I can worship You again.

All of creation owes to You

Our existence and our praise

You are the Word of the Father

Without You nothing was made that was made.

Thank You, oh Yahshua,

Mediator, standard of righteousness

Your promises stand forever,

High Priest of the Zadokim.

Part III:
Identity

Part III: Identity

Sparkle, Shine, Oh Star of Mine

Sparkle, shine, oh star of Mine

Steadily light the way

A star in the night is the promise of light

The certainty of a new day.

Steady on, celestial one

Let anointed trumpets blow

Hear, oh ears, the resounding of years

Let all the people know.

There is hope in the darkness

There is rest in the breeze

There is peace in the comfort of home

There is truth in the speaking

And silence in ease

But My light shall carry you on.

Whether traipsing through sand

Or on rocky, hard ground

And in walking on water, too

There is something surer than what you have found

Much deeper than what you can do.

Reality's strong under illusory earth

What you see is not really what is

But close tight your eyes and see with your heart

A Truth that just cannot be missed.

There is peace in the battle

There's rest in the storm

I've comforted, "Peace, be still!"

Take your eyes off the water

The swirling harsh swarm

I'm still sleeping, so all is well.

Sparkle and shine, oh steady on light

Forget not where you are from

When you are surrounded by cold, endless night

You're really surrounded by Love.

And as you receive it and as you believe it

You shine all the brighter still

So that others can see and then come to be

Shining stars themselves.

As you've heard My Word, so you shall be heard

Sending My Promise on forth

A strong steady light in others' long nights

So be with Me, just stay the course.

Sparkle, shine, oh star of Mine

You give Me great delight

For you are what I saw before time

And I've placed you here, tonight.

Part III: Identity

Oh Mighty Zadokim

Oh mighty Zadokim,

Which from my Presence flows,

Now I have made you clean,

I've given you new robes

The righteousness of Christ

And a crown upon your head

Peace within your heart

A joy that doesn't end

Oh mighty Zadokim,

Oh mighty son of Mine

Bearing the image of your Father

And the message of the Christ

You minister to me,

Offering the fat and blood,

And in My Presence you receive

My offering of love

Oh mighty Zadokim,

Oh mighty river flow

I've given you new wings

New places so to go

You shall soar on to new heights

You shall grow like never before

You shall inherit a son's rights

You shall stand at My front door

Calling all to enter in,

Having pressed in to My heart

You are My loyal Zadokim

Knowing firmly Who You Are

Oh mighty Zadokim

I've called you now to shine

But I've seen this all along,

For I knew you before time

I have seen it, I believed it

I have made it to be so

I am pleased that you've received it

Keep believing 'til you know

Righteous, mighty Zadokim

Holy, purposed son of Mine

I bless you now with life and peace

And I send you out to shine.

Zadokim

The priests, the Levites, the sons of Zadok,

Who uphold the Law of Love

May enter His Presence and minister there

May offer Him the fat and the blood

We have the privilege to offer our lives

To give Yahweh everything

To worship Him fully with all that we are

To glorify Him as our King

There is no blockage 'tween Yahweh and us

He will not send us away

We can come before Him, and with Him we sup

Our lives worship Him every day

We may be with our Father, we may be ourselves,

Who we were before time even began

We are true to reality, purposed in love

We shall worship again and again

We are able to be with our Father

Able to give Him all things!

Is there a better honor?

Is there a better way?

Praise Yahweh for giving us access

Yahshua for shedding the blood

That we may draw near to our Father

Abiding in His endless love!

We get to minister to Yahweh

Our deepest desire fulfilled

And we get to live in His Presence

Where we were before He made the world

We are the sons of our Father,

Sons of the righteous One

And what's in His heart is our value

For we are faithful sons.

Chosen

What an honor to be Abraham

Chosen before time

To build a mighty nation

That dwells in grace sublime.

What an honor to be David

Chosen to be king

To bring Yahweh's will

To Israel

And all the Psalms to sing.

What an honor to be Mary

Chosen to bear Christ

A simple girl

That heard the Word

And brought the world new life.

What an honor to be me

Chosen of my God

To be brought into righteousness

That I will not be lost.

And what an honor to be chosen

To bring into creation

What Yahweh hoped for

Longed to bring

Through this generation.

You

You know who you are

You have a pedigree

Your name has been inscribed

In places heavenly.

Who you are will never change

By what you feel or do

Circumstances cannot alter

What Yahweh knows to be true.

You know who you are!

You have a pedigree!

Yahweh birthed you from His heart

Then He came and set you free!

From His Spirit deep inside you

He is teaching you to trust

Like a child trusting a Father

Knowing His Word is enough.

You know who you are!

For He's telling you Himself

You're the one He came back for

For you He sacrificed Himself.

You know who you are!

Yahweh has made you whole

There can be no doubt of

All you really need to know.

You are Yahweh's beloved

You are His precious child

You are the one He died for

You're the one who He inspired.

You're the one He wants to work through

You're the one He's given power

And He never will desert you

When you have a needful hour.

You're the one Yahweh entrusted

With your life and assignment

You're the one He loved ere time began

And you're the one He sent.

You show others what He looks like

For His image you do bear

And when people look at your life

They can't help but see Him there.

You're the one who gives Him glory

You're the one through whom He shines

You're the one who lives the story

That He's written line by line.

You've been registered in Heaven

All creation knows your name

You shall stand upon the mountaintop

And Yahweh you will proclaim.

Son of the only Father

Who sent His only begotten Son

To make other sons and fathers

To make many out of One.

You're the one creation hopes for

With groans it cannot express

You're the mighty one of Yahweh

And He's given you His rest.

You speak what Yahweh's spoken

You have faith to make it seen

The world has not been broken

Because it Yahweh has redeemed.

You're the one with eyes to see

And you're the one with ears to hear

You have the faith to believe

So you need to have no fear.

You know who you are!

You have a pedigree!

You've been registered in Heaven

Creation listens when you speak.

Purpose

You can make a difference

Just by being who you are

While man looks at the outside,

Yahweh's looking at the heart

Spirit calls out to spirit

And deep calls out to deep

Whether or not you hear it

Yahweh's setting people free

They may never come and thank you

But they're seeing your light shine

You may never know the impact

That you've had on someone's life

But have faith that you are shining

And that Yahweh's working through

The light that you're emitting,

Calling to His people in you

So keep walking in your purpose,

Just keep being who you are

Yahweh sees your contribution

And He's beaming oh so hard

He is smiling and delighting

In who He made you to be

He is opening the eyes of those

Who have the faith to see

May your eyes today be opened

To the beauty that is you

May you grow in faith and hope

May you see your own light, too

Steady on, oh bright one

Let your anointed graces flow

Who you are in the Father

Cannot help but show

Resting in the promise

That Yahweh has made to you

That you are making a difference,

You're a blessing and that's huge.

Stolen, Recovered

It started as a whisper, but soon became a shout

A shout that was heard throughout the ages

"Yahweh doesn't love you, hasn't given you all things

Everything you need for generations."

Because the first lie wasn't that you would be like gods

That you would have the wisdom of the Father

The first lie was implicit in that statement above:

That we weren't like Yahweh, that we were "other."

But we didn't have to eat of the fruit to be like God

We didn't have to partake of that tree

Because we always were One with Yahweh God

And how could we any more like Him be?

But they believed the lie, the man and woman both

And when they took the fruit of separation

They brought about the curse that all creation knows

And with the axe of lies brought condemnation.

And thousands upon thousands of years had come and gone

And people born in every generation

Never realized what had truly been lost

Because the enemy brought separation.

But then one precious day, Yahshua came to Earth

To bring us back into the Truth again

He came because He wanted creation to unfold

The way Yahweh intended when it began.

And on the cross He died, showing us His love

Showing us there WASN'T separation

In dying, He brought life, and He made us One

Uniting us again as His Creation.

But the enemy, that liar, continued to speak

Into the hearts of the stewards of creation

Saying Yahweh didn't really want us to be His

That all there ever was was separation.

But how could this be so, us not One with Him?

How could we be other than united?

When everybody knows lie isn't creation

That only TRUTH can be and truth is righteous

There is no separation, there's only unity

For only Yahweh's Word can create

On each day of Creation Yahweh said, "Let it be"

And Word and Spirit carried out Heaven's mandate.

And so I write this poem, some rumors to dispel

Rumors that aroused a righteous anger

Yahweh loves us truly; Yahweh loves us well

And being separate never was a danger.

Authority

Why not believe

That in any situation you walk into,

You are graced and empowered to be Yahweh's glory in the Earth

Why not believe

That everything that's happening around you

Can work together in Yahweh to benefit and bless you,

Redemption of all that was cursed

Why not believe

That Yahweh sees majesty and beauty

Whenever He looks and who He has made you to be

Why not believe

That He has given you all authority

To declare and decree what He has been longing to see

If we believe

In the power of the Christ that dwells within us,

We can look in the mirror and see only Him in the glass

We can let go

Of the lies that the enemy has told us

That we are not worthy and conquer the sins of the past

Then we can be

The kings and priests of Yahweh's ecclesia

Growing the Kingdom and walking with Him day by day

But only if we

Submit to the vision of the glory

The hope of the Christ in the Earth, in our hearts, in today.

So yes, believe!

Believe the Word that Yahweh has spoken

That He made you to be His glory, His power in the Earth

Just like our elder brother,

Yahshua who walked here before us

We carry out the Father's heart, His will, His holy purpose.

Value

The life in a seed

The currents in an ocean

The wind in the leaves

The glory in the chosen.

It's the purpose in a dream

The whisper in a promise

The joy in the peace

The Christ that is in us.

It's the rest in the battle

The faith in a word

The voice in the darkness

Bringing light to the world.

The victory in silence

The Truth that's redeemed

The joy set before Him

The reason for being.

The treasure within

These vessels of Earth

The inherent redemption

From that which was cursed.

The garden of Eden

That great promised land

The ability to walk

With Yahweh hand in hand.

Heaven and Earth

Together as One.

The universe in one heart

The bride that says "Come!"

The Creator placed value

In His creation

"Evaluate us, Yahweh!

Let it be not masked by sin!"

Inherent and internal

It's always been there

We manifest our own value

The Christ which we bear.

Somebody Has to Say Yes

Sometimes,

It is easy to think that I am not important

In the grand scheme of things.

That You, omnipotent, and able to redeem

All things together for good

Do not need little me

That I don't matter

Why should I be?

But somebody has to say yes

You've been waiting and waiting for someone to come

Somebody who would say, "Yes, I believe You, My Father, and all

that You've called me to be."

And that's me.

That's me.

Yahweh, I say, YES

And Amen

Amen to Your promises

I will believe You

Yes and Amen

I receive all Your Word, I will walk in the Earth

I will be

The hope of Christ's glory

And all that You called me to be

When You first envisioned me and said let it be.

Yes and Amen.

A Walking Revelation

I'm resting in the knowledge of My God Most High

And here beneath the Branches of the Tree of Life

I receive a fruit that will never die

And become a living witness of Eternal Life

I see into the Garden where it all began

And so my heart is called into my Promised Land

There redeeming seed of the Son of Man

To become a testimony of the Great I AM

My purpose I won't forfeit, it goes ever on

And I am a witness—A Faithful son

The blessing of My Father is to be well done

A walking revelation of the Holy One.

Part IV:
The Heavens Declare

I Know Why Creation Sings

I know why the brook babbles flowing over rocks

I know why birds sing flying in great flocks

I know why the wind whistles through trees

I know why creation sings!

I know why cats purr, I know why babies coo

I know why there's a sound for everything we do

I know why dogs bark and wolves howl at the moon

All creation sings for joy: Yahshua's coming soon!

Every breath, every blink, every heartbeat cries

All of Yahweh's creation as a witness testifies

And yet who sings louder than I, for I join this symphony

All creation sings as One in perfect harmony.

A Halo Surrounds the Moon

Sometimes the nights are long, cold, and lonely

And I don't know how to reach the morning

But when I look up at the night sky

I see what I could never see in daylight.

There in the darkness the moon shall arise

And all around it a halo of light

Millions and billions of stars in the sky

Show that Yahweh my God is still king of the night.

A heavenly host of stars shining bright

And the great star that produces daylight

All always shining up in the sky

Ever unwavering rays of right.

There in the darkness the moon shall arise

And all around it a halo of light

Millions and billions of stars in the sky

Show that Yahweh my God is king of all light.

For there is no difference between night and day

Sun, moon, and stars shine brightly always

Eternal and constant, the bright morning star

In the Radiance of Yahweh we find who we are.

The Butterfly

A caterpillar looks around, instinctively he knows

It's time to lay its life down, let the old things go

But darkness looms ahead for him, and fear roars in his ears

He's not sure he will make it through; he could just stay right here.

Cocoons are hard! he thinks inside. Dark, dreary, and enclosed,

I will have to go and hide inside of it alone.

I want to be a butterfly, but I don't know if I can;

It isn't safe! his heart does cry. Is it worth it in the end?

Oh how I'm like the caterpillar, looking only at circumstance

If I looked at the butterfly, I'd gladly take a chance

For butterflies have wings to fly, to soar amongst the heights

But to get wings, I have to die, for day comes through the night.

So I will gaze at the butterfly and enter my cocoon

I will trust the deep desire birthed inside my womb

I'll set my eyes upon the joy waiting before me now

And I will sing inside the dark and keep the peace somehow.

Oh, I will be a butterfly, emerging you will see

The splendor and the glory that was always meant for me

For Yahweh, He did hide inside great and colorful things

But if I stay a caterpillar, you'll never see the wings.

A Promise to a Caterpillar (Who Is a Butterfly)

A dash of hope, a smidge of peace, a heaping bowl of joy,

I have made you so complete, I've given you wings to soar

A splash of red, the brightest orange, the yellow shining bright

Such beauty! On these wings you'll fly and show the world My light.

The way is open now to you, the air is free and clear

You know exactly how to do that for which I've called you here

I've given you the space to be, ascending to new heights

Unlimited, I set you free in the wide expansive skies.

Sing your songs and shout your praise, let what's in shine without

I've given you a set of days, my business to be about

Express what I have placed in you, allow yourself to shine

Look inside and see the heart, that spark of the divine.

Show the world what can only be when you and I relate

Together we have perfect peace, together we create

Look only at Me and My promises, don't look upon the dirt

For I made you above to live, not crawl upon the earth.

Be who you are, I created you to express the joy I feel

When I look at you just being you, when I see your precious zeal

The passion that you have for me is only surpassed by

The love that I have when I see you using your wings to fly.

You have always been a butterfly, even when small and slimy and green

The caterpillar stage was just a time to mature you in all things

So go! And be the butterfly I created you to be

I promise even as you fly, you'll always be with Me.

Sunrise

Did the sun rise today?

Good, Yahweh is faithful.

I am only asked to stand in faith

On days in which the sun has risen.

Are there stars in the sky?

Good, Yahweh is faithful.

I am only asked to stand in faith

When the stars are in the sky.

Did Yahweh speak a Word?

Good, Yahweh is faithful.

I am only asked to stand

On the Word that He has spoken

And has, undoubtedly,

Already brought to pass.

I am only asked to stand

on the faith that is

The fullness of Yahweh,

Who is Faithful.

Flight

Today I watched a hawk in flight

Wings outstretched in graceful glide

Slight adjustments to the wings

To meet air currents, nothing big

But currents change and wind does blow

Suddenly, height was becoming low

So wings did flap, the bird ascended

But the flight had not yet ended

For there, again, in a pocket of air

The hawk did soar without a care

Oh the perspective he must see

When not concentrating on his wings

And I imagined this is life,

To soar quite high above the strife

Oh, winds will change, bluster, and blow

But with a flap of the wings, away we'll go

For Yahweh's given us a gift

He gave us thrust, dynamics, lift

He gave us wings on which to soar

Because He wants to show us more

Ascending, descending heights to see

And we shall arise on steady wings

For we, like hawks, know how to fly

And look Reality in the eye.

Night

What do you mean,

The night is dark and lonely?

Do you not see

What I have made you to be?

You are the star

Shining bright in the sky

Just by who you are

You illuminate the night

You are a promise

Of light to the Earth

When surrounded by darkness

You remind it of its worth

For though you are a star

I have given you a Sun

He is my Morning Star

And you point to the One

He makes the daylight,

But you shine in the dark

So you always have light

No matter where you are

And you are not the only star

I've given to the world

The host of heaven stretches far

My glory to unfurl

So the night is never dark,

At least it's not for you

When you remember who you are

And let My glory through

And you never are alone

You're in a constellation

I've given you a place, a home

Among a holy nation

A people who will know their worth

And shine from deep within

A people who will radiate

A people who will win.

Part V:
Tools for Triumph

My Life Is a Series of Triumphs

My life is a series of triumphs

Of battles fought and won

My life is a series of victories

Of issues with which I'm done

My life is a thing of beauty

Of ever increasing grace

My life is a thing of righteousness

As I walk with Yahweh by faith

My life is a thing of purpose

It's no mystery why I am here

Yahweh has called me to choose Him

And I do so without fear

My life is a serious message

Showing Yahweh's most glorious gift

For He can take one who was dying

And give her the strength to live

My life is much more than my lifetime

As I manifest Yahweh's Word

For centuries, millennia after I'm gone

My life's consequences shall be heard

My life is a glorious Promise

To myself and to all who can see

A Promise from a Father to His faithful son

That what He says is all that shall be.

Hope

Today I saw once again

How cruel life can be

To those who are just starting out in it,

To the innocent,

Those who didn't do anything to deserve it

And how horrible, how utterly horrible

Was the fall from grace

That brought us here

To this place

Of hope and fear and

Lack of strength

It's been so long since I've seen

True and lasting joy,

But I think I saw a glimpse of it once,

Brief flashes of ecstasy

In a world of agony

And the promise of a lasting peace,

A lasting truth and righteousness

And joy

I look at the world and I can see

The obviousness of the agony

Children who live in daily fear,

Who hurt themselves and others because

That's all they've ever seen,

All they've ever known

All they've ever felt:

Unwanted and alone

And they've never had a place

To call their own

And I remember when I felt that way,

Ten years ago,

And yesterday

And I'm faced with a choice again,

That choice to stay here and submit

To the chaos and darkness and to the fall

To the horrors of circumstances

And what I see every day

Every day

Every

Single

Day

But I can choose to arise,

Ascend

To see more than merely circumstance

To look at myself and know

I am better than I was

They can be better too,

We can be better too,

The world will get better, too

Because Yahweh...

So I will choose to hope recklessly,

Irrationally,

I will choose to have a hope that makes people go,

"What the heck?"

When they look at me

The hope that has always been inside of me

And causes me to keep going,

Keep going, keep going

The hope that, in spite of the pain and the agony,

The "Please let it stop!" and the certainty that

There's no way I can hold on for one

More

Second

And yet I will not give up

I will not quit

I will keep on

Because I don't want to miss anything

And I'm sure,

Just so sure,

Just so sure,

That it must get better in the end

And perhaps the next victory is just around the corner.

Notice

This is just to say.

I WILL NOT QUIT!

No way...

Whatever may happen,

No matter what

I will walk out my purpose

In faith and trust

For I clearly hear Yahweh

And know what will be

So NOTE to the world:

My purpose you'll see!

Weapons

I take the light and pierce the darkness

With the Truth I skewer lies

In righteousness I slay wrongness

I triumph over death with life.

By faith I create a new thing

And in love I nations birth

I operate by power of Yahweh

Upheld in eternity by His Word.

In peace and rest I shall rise up

Abiding in Infinity

I call all other powers silenced

Yahweh sets all creation free.

Treasure Hunt

Righteousness, peace, and joy in His love

Purpose and passion and grace

The knowledge that I am always enough

Life more abundantly, faith

Promises spoken ere time ever began

Gifts and talents, too

Planted as seeds in the mind of each man

Combinations that make you you

Though they may be hidden, 'neath life's circumstance

Though they may be hard to find,

If we can participate in the divine dance

We'll find treasure inside of our mind

Whatever may happen to us in this life,

Yahweh's Word is always in play

The firmest foundation on which we can thrive

The soil out of which grows each day

The Word of our God can supersede all

But we may have to go dig around

The Garden of Eden wasn't destroyed by the fall

Just hidden under rocky ground

Perfection, Yahweh's pleasure, a treasure inside

In each of us, Yahweh does dwell

And all of His gifts still inside of our minds

Waiting safely, protected, and well.

Just in My Head

You say that it's all "just in my head"

But in my head are worlds, and if like Einstein said

The thoughts in my head become reality

Then what's in my head is soon to be seen

It's all about having the mind of Christ,

You see, it's important to renew the mind

For what's in our head is what we create

And the world doesn't need to see anger and hate

So fixing our eyes on things above,

Renewing the mind with visions of love

Trying and trying to overcome

What's "just in my head" is hard enough

But society says what's inside doesn't count

It's what you do outside, what's in should be out

But society lies, it cannot understand

Every seed in good soil produces in the end

What my thoughts show me now, if I nurture you'll see

So if I'm plowing the ground in my head, let me be

Each of us has a responsibility

To take charge of our minds and shape reality.

Knowing

Sometimes I feel that I am being chopped into thousands of little

pieces stroke by stroke with one sharp, two-edged sword

But more importantly,

I know You'll put me back together again.

Sometimes I feel that I am being held underwater so long that I will

drown before I can get one more breath

But more importantly,

I know You are the Breath of Life in me.

Sometimes I feel that I can't walk even one more step, and that to

try will make me fall to the floor

But more importantly,

I know Your Word is to keep going.

Sometimes I feel like I can't do this anymore

But more importantly,

I know it's already done.

Righteous Anger

I am angry, there is no excuse

Babylon, quit refusing to lose

There is no reason, this is not right!

People should not have to live in these lies!

There should be no doubting,

No troublesome minds

We should not sink lower

Than glorious heights

There should be no sorrow, suffering, or hate

Holy Spirit's oath puts an end to debate

Brood of vipers, villainous curs,

Get thee gone or hear the Word!

Line up with the Spirit, it's time for the light

Babylon no longer has any hold on my mind

And the Truth of the vision, this truth shall be told

Babylon no longer has any stronghold!

I'm tired of battles, tired of the fight

Tired of darkness pervading the night

Yahshua's the victor, it's already won

Come celebrate, army of the faithful sons!

See the vision clearly, see with the heart

What if the night was never meant to be dark?

What if night was purposed for the glory of Yahweh?

There are more suns at night than there are during the day.

Daylight's a vision of victory come

But night's the same battle, it's already won

The sun is a promise of life to the Earth

The stars are a sign of impending birth

The same light shines within us

That shines in the Son

For we are the stars

And we are the ones

We see the promise, the daylight within

We've laid hold of what darkness cannot comprehend

So, devil, keep on pushing, I know you won't win

'Cause I'll go freaking supernova if you try this again!

What I Have Never Seen

I've never seen a happy life
One that is more freedom than pain,
I've never seen a person light,
And walking unafraid.

I've always lived upon the edge,
Fearing one mistake
For if I do but one thing wrong,
Everyone will me forsake.

I've never seen a place of safety
Where all are on my side
No matter what I do or don't
They will not me deride.

I've never had a place to call home
A place where I am loved
Loved without condition
And I know that I'm enough.

I've always had a question,
Always wondered if there's more
If there's a God who loves me,
Will He open wide the door?

Will He gather me up to Him?

Will He give me now a home?

Can I have a place of hope and rest?

Will He call me now His own?

Will He give me what I've never seen?

What I have never known?

Will He bequeath to me my deepest dream?

Can I be aught but alone?

But I believe, though I've not seen,

There's more than what there is

And so one day I will receive

A life that's truly His.

I will not fear to mess it up,

Won't fear being abandoned

I will rest now in endless love

And let go of what I can't do.

I have faith, though I've not seen

And so I'm truly blessed

I cannot fail, I will succeed

For I am Yahweh's best.

Triumph

Every Goliath we face

Will one day be a bear

And every bear we've slain

Was once Goliath

So we are now victorious

We need only be aware

And face whatever we face

In sure triumph

I have slain the giant!

I have killed the one

Who tried to come against

My sacred calling

And all I had to do

Was see things as a son

To know that Babylon's

Already fallen.

For My Students

Yahweh is the God of an entire host of armies,

A nation of angels for every child

In Yahweh is everything that each child needs

Comfort to embrace them, to tame what is wild.

Oh Yahweh my God, You are with them right now

Whether or not they have eyes to see

I speak that they can have eyes somehow

The miracle of mercy, the Truth that does free.

I speak over them safety, life, and abundance

That they'll persevere in the dark 'til light shines

And then when their eyes are open in wonder

They'll forget the pain of all terrible times.

Yahweh I see, my door has been opened

Now I can open a door for them too

Yahweh I kneel, I unleash a fountain

A river of life flowing to them from You.

Part V: Tools for Triumph

The In Between

It is that I live in the in between

Seeing more than is normally seen

On one side or another, a grander view

Of what Yahweh has spoken, of what is true.

In between the heavens and the Earth

In between the completion and the curse

In between groups of people that I know

In between what is seen and what is known.

Oh! To stand in the in between

Is not as easy as it may seem

Sometimes I feel very much alone

But intercessors must have a place to groan.

Are others here in the in between?

Can others see what I have seen?

Yahweh's vision and Yahweh's sight

A light in the darkness, day in the night?

I know they are there, the others who see

But right now they're far, far away from me

And I feel alone in the in between

Separated from those whose eyes have not seen.

But oh, what options are left to me now

Closing tight my eyes, keeping the vision out?

If I did not see, if I did not know

The visions that Yahweh does to me show.

Why, then I'd be dead, that I know full well

There's no life without Yahweh, no place to dwell

For it's here that I find Him, it's here that I see

Here the revelation, the joy, and the peace.

It's here I find purpose and promises sure

It's here I find strength to stand on the Word

It is here I can journey to where I've begun

It's here I am growing yet already done.

In the in between, I, intercessor arise

For the one in between can see on both sides

Can show to the other what's always been there

Can stand with his brother and lift up his prayer.

Can whisper the promises of life to the world

Can write a true poem of glory unfurled

Can fight in a battle that's already won

Can stand with the Father a true, righteous son.

Is the in between worth it? Absolutely, I'm sure!

I would not trade it now for a thing in the world

For in between what was, what is, and shall be

We shine forth Yahweh's promises so all can see!

So come to the in between, see for yourself

Meet the Vision Caster, stand with Him, and help

Help all those whose eyes have been closed in the night

To see Yahweh's visions, to dance in the light.

The in between is special and not all choose to go

But it's worth it, I promise, I want you to know

It's the place with the Father, the place of a son

It's the place He can finish what He's already done.

Part VI: Poetry and Parables

Poetry and Parables

In poetry and parables,
I speak more than just one Word
The gift wrapping of mysteries
In parables and poetry

In parables and poetry
I can give you eyes to see
Read it once, come back again
See it anew, alright, begin

In poetry and parables,
I with language frame the world
Within, find healing for the soul
For with My Word I've made you whole

The dark storm rises, chopping fright
Obscurity casts out the light
And fear causes trembling from within
But I have come to conquer sin

The depths of longing swallow deep
But I have promises to keep
And I can raise a thousand sheep
And find just one alone, asleep

The heights of ecstasy can enthrall
Leave you feeling ten feet tall
With heart wide open you can see
Your way home and back to Me

The depths of sorrow pull you down
You gasp for air, so sure you'll drown
But if you stop and look around
You'll see I've always kept you safe and sound

The poetry of life is grand
I know, I shaped it with my hand
The Greatest Story Ever Told
So let this poem make you bold

Each time you look at your life again
I'll let you see it with a new lens
Don't perish for lack of true vision
With eyes to see, do enter in

Read your own poem, you parable
In you I've made the whole world full
But see it true and see it right
Open your eyes and be the light

For everyone with eyes to see
Their parable, their poetry
Will find a different side of Me
Each time they open up to read.

Part VI: Poetry and Parables

A Love Story

What if someone loves you so much

That he decided to write a whole story

A great Novel to prove to you

Exactly how much he loves you

A story with a beautiful ending

A glorious ending

The most happy ending

That exceeds your wildest dreams

Yet was born inside his mind

Dreamed up and created and laid out

Just for you

And what if he had the power

To make this story come to life?

To lay it out before you as a path for you to walk on

Your life

Every high and low, every mountain and valley

Every twist and turn

Leading you back to him

And to that happy ending that is beyond

Far beyond

Your deepest heart's desire

This is your life

Yahweh's epic love story,

Written just for you.

The Poetry of the Plan

How beautiful are words, worlds of sound and meaning

Spoken or just written on a page

And when they're called aloud, how beautiful the Being

For by His Word the universe is made

But more beautiful still are words that come to order

In Yahweh's plan of poetry arranged

And in this plan we see the mystery before us

Glory revealed as each Word takes its place

The poetry that purpose does dictate.

Ode to And

Such a beautiful word
Conjunction
Joining two things that,
Upon first glance
Seem separate
But really, they are
One.

Faith and hope

Love and grace

Fire and peace

Joy and flame.

Joining
Heaven and Earth
Creator and Creation
Each individual birth
To every nation.
Joining that which is
To that which will be
Joining Yahweh to all He made
And you to me.

Poetry

A verse, a line, a song to your spirit

To remind you once again

Of the promise of the Father

Something He spoke into being before time ever began

Yourself

And everything

Infinite-eternity wrapped up

In a verse, a line, a song

Truth shot to the heart

An arrow that does not miss

A Word that does not return void

A Promise

Oh, how marvelous, how glorious!

To be a poet.

Part VII: Heartsongs

Heart's Cry

I want to bask in Your glorious presence

See the truth of who I am

I want to dance among the heavens

As I walk upon the land

I want to sing a song of glory,

Experience rebirth

I want to tell my Father's story

Bring the Heavens to the Earth

I want to elevate my Father,

To bring glory to His Name

I want to share His Truth with others

So that they can do the same

I want to whisper to the Father

Sing praises in His ear

I want to worship Him forever

Not caring who else hears

I have a longing deep inside me

With my Father to be One

I want to come out of hiding

Be exposed as Yahweh's son

Oh my deepest heart's desire,

So fundamental to my being

To always belong to Yahweh

And for Him to speak to me

But the longing of my heart's cry

Goes deeper than this still,

Beyond mere explanation

And more than words can tell

The utterances within me

Groans that words cannot express

Voice the longing deep inside me

To receive Yahweh's fullness

But my Father heard my heartsong

Echoing through time and space

And He made a sure provision

He prepared for me a place

So profoundly does my heart cry

But in the end all is well

For my Father heard my longing

And gave me in Him a place to dwell.

Part VII: Heartsongs

Breathe

The deepest desires of my inner being

To enter Your Presence and there within be

To pass through the portal and open the door

To be with my Father forever once more

The greatest desires of my truest heart

To abide in You, Father, never to part

To be caught up in Your glory, to live there within

To read Your authored story, to once again live

Passing through the darkness and into the light,

Once again I find myself caught up in a fight

I don't know if I'll make it, but I must somehow

Because I know that You're worth it and I need You now

Caught up in the struggle, I sometimes forget

I don't need to struggle; it's fixed so I win

I don't have to fight now to come back to You

For You came back for me, yes me You did choose

Remembering to trust you, the struggles do cease

And finally I can receive perfect peace

Entering Your Presence beyond blinding veil

Receiving equipping so I never fail

And I breathe You in, I abide with You

You're the oxygen to my dying Truth

And I know again Who You are to me

You're my Father, I'm Your Son, and I'm free

Then arise worry, fearing, and doubt

Why would You ever want me and not cast me out?

Everyone's always hated me, do You the same?

Why would You take me and call me by name?

Questions without answers, I'm asking again

But answers don't matter when Yahweh's within

The Truth supersedes the lies born of fear

When it can't be explained, it's still real; You're still here

And I breathe You in, and You soothe my soul

I know once again that You've made me whole

Please just hold me tight and stay by my side

Everything's alright if we just abide

So, Father, my Father, be with me always

I will stay in Your Presence; I will live in Your faith

Believing the unseen, impossible dreams

I will receive the victory; I will have perfect peace

I will breathe in Your essence, my heart beat to Your heart

I will revel in Your presence; I will know who You are

I will dance to a melody that's only my own

I will rest in my family; I will live in my home.

The End-All-Be-All

If I have a loving family—a devoted husband

And well-behaved children

Maybe a pet or two

In a nice, cozy house,

But have not Yahweh,

I have nothing

If I have a rewarding job where I make a difference

Have a future, good benefits,

A nice salary with options

And a convenient location

But have not Yahweh,

I lack all

If I have all the things—a big house and a car

Vacations every year

All the latest conveniences

And money to spare

But have not Yahweh

I am only temporarily enjoying what can never last.

Yahweh is righteousness, Yahweh is joy

He is peace, love, and the light in the darkness.

Yahweh is everything! The first and last, everlasting to everlasting.

Yahweh never fails.

But where people are fickle and things disappear

This one thing remains

Always, there is Yahweh, the Greatest Above Anything.

Return to Me the Missing Pieces

In one act of rebellion

Creation did divide

Shattered into pieces

And scattered far and wide.

Ever since that day,

Ever since that time,

On each and every heart

Has been one single cry:

"Return to me, Oh Yahweh,

That in You I can stand

Let me be Your child

And redeem Your land

Make me whole forever

Make me new again

Return to me the pieces

That were scattered in the wind."

And Yahweh, He did hear

The cry of each man's heart

He understood their passion

Not to be apart.

He sent to us the Word

To redeem and restore

To return the pieces

And join them all once more.

"I return to You, Creation

That in Me you can stand

You shall be My children

And redeem My land

I make you whole forever

I've made you new again

I return to You the pieces

That were scattered in the wind."

But this was not surprising

For though 'twas man's desire

The heart of man is not

From whence began the fire.

It began in Yahweh,

His Spirit burning bright

He calls the missing pieces

To be set aright.

"Return to me, My pieces,

That in you I can stand

Be unto Me, My People

And I shall be your Lamb

I will sacrifice Him

To make us One again,

For You are not just pieces

You are my Zadokim."

Arise, Shine (See and Become Radiant)

From Isaiah 60

See, and become radiant

Let your heart be filled with joy

Look upon the mountains,

Upon the mountains of Yahweh

And let us shine in the darkness

Shine upon this great land

For His glory is on us

And we're upheld by His right hand

So we praise, HalleluYah!

So we worship His name

So we praise, HalleluYah!

Forever in faith, forever in grace

Let all proclaim the praises of Yahweh

Let all ascend to His altar

For He has glorified the house of His glory

And He'll bring His sons from afar

So we praise, HalleluYah!

So we worship His name

So we praise, HalleluYah!

Forever in faith, forever in grace

And He has called the city of Yahweh

Zion, His holy place

The walls are salvation

And the gates, we are praise

So we praise, HalleluYah!

So we worship His name

So we praise, HalleluYah!

Forever in faith, forever in grace.

Beyond the Laws of Space and Time

Beyond the laws of space and time

We dance the dance of the divine

Communing with our Father's heart

Receiving what He has to impart

Seated on the throne of grace

Looking into the Father's face

Knowing all that He has made

Is more than what we can explain

A new dimension we can see

A broader view of the tapestry

If we expand the vision shown

Beyond all that we've ever known

Beyond the laws of time and space

Above the Earth and all the days

The ancient and Eternal One

Speaks to the hearts of His chosen sons

He shows us more than we understand

But we can trust His glorious plan

We know the purpose He has for us

And knowing Him, we have enough

A new dimension we can see

A broader view of the tapestry

If we expand the vision shown

Beyond all that we've ever known

For our hearts are to glorify the Father

Our minds are to serve Him once again

We shall be what He did see

When He spoke us into being and said, "Amen."

A new dimension we can see

A broader view of the tapestry

If we expand the vision shown

Beyond all that we've ever known.

The Tenth Leper

Once there was a leper

Whose life was surely hell

He walked in a world that wouldn't

Allow him therein to dwell

Until one day he was walking

Along a dusty road

And He met the Messiah

Who made him to be whole

There were nine other lepers

Who were all healed too

But this tenth leper was the only one

Who seemed to have a clue

"Oh thank you dear Messiah!"

And at His feet he fell

"Arise and go your way," He said,

"Your faith has made you well."

But this was just one leper

And there were many more

Who thought that they were surely

Beating down death's door

Many people cried

And healing they demanded

But would they give their lives

As was so commanded?

But those of us who

Will our lives sacrifice

Can rest in assurance that

He'll make everything right

"Oh thank you dear Messiah!"

Each of our hearts will swell

"Arise and go your way," He'll say,

"Your faith has made you well."

I remember when

I lived in earthly hell

I thought that I could never

Escape that nether realm

But then one day a knowing

Began to grow inside

And what was only glowing

Burst forth into light

And I received a freedom

I never knew was there

And I'll always be grateful

For the healing He prepared

"Oh thank you dear Messiah!"

And great tears of joy fell

"Arise and go your way," He said,

"Your faith has made you well."

Once I Was Broken

I will always be grateful

For the ability to feel joy

For once I was broken

And felt nothing but deep sadness and mind-numbing pain

I will never take for granted

The ability to walk or use my limbs

For once I was broken

And couldn't even bend a finger

I will always feel delighted at

A calm, steady heartbeat

For once I was broken

And panic would make my heart race almost daily

I will always enjoy

The energy that flows through my body

For once I was broken

And didn't even feel strong enough to face another day

I will always be grateful

For a family of believers

For once I was broken

And did not know that people could ever be on your side

I will always marvel

At the ability to relate to the God who created everything

Always wonder that He wants to relate to me,

Be with me,

That He loves me and even

Delights in me

For once I was broken

And I did not think I was even worthy to live

I will always cherish my life

For once I was broken

And the enemy told me I would always be broken

And tried to get me to die

I will always be grateful

That I am not broken

Because Yahweh promised me I wouldn't be

And once I was broken

But oh, the greatness of the glory,

The ability to say "once, but no longer"

For once I was broken,

And Yahweh fixed me.

Offering

Today I walk in places that I never thought to go

I have people who love me, in my Father I am home

I see the vision clearly, I have purpose, I have faith

I love my Father dearly, I walk in glory and in grace

I've come through many battles and I've come through many wars

But I never won a battle until I learned to lay down my sword

Receiving what was offered when my Father called me son

I learned to hear the called Word and abide in Yahweh's love

A New Covenant was spoken before time even began

It's this Covenant I walk in as I rest in Yahweh's hands

To glorify my Father is the cry of my own heart

And I know it now is possible as I learn to impart

But I never could've gotten here, I never would've known

Never would've received peace or any glory shown

If the Father hadn't offered it, if He did not hold out His hand

If He didn't come back to redeem His people and His land

If Yahshua did not hear His Father and obey His voice

And lay His life upon a cross by His own righteous choice

If Holy Spirit did not dwell within and teach us Yahweh's ways

If there was no Law from Heaven that Yahweh made to keep us safe

Wherever I am the Kingdom is, wherever I go Yahweh's promise

Shines brightly forth in the emptiness, the hope that creation will harness

To continue on until Yahweh comes, to keep going 'til all is redeemed

For He's already here in His faithful sons, He already lives here in me

I offer my life to my Father as He offered His life to me

I know He is pleased with this offering and how proud He is to receive

What's offered cannot be accepted until it's offered with a full heart

Praise Yahweh for offering His Kingdom; He is where offering starts

Now we offer a promise to creation as Yahweh's righteous kings

We promise His worth and His vision, His righteousness, joy, and His peace:

Wherever you go He shall find you, wherever you are, He shall be

He will most surely remind you of your identity

He'll show you the vision of Truth, that from the beginning He made

He'll show the place He had for you, when He first set out to create

Receive the Promise by faith, become the Promise yourself

I tell you He is worth it all and your heart will finally be filled.

ABOUT THE AUTHOR

Cassondra Beers is a living representation of Yahweh in the Earth. She is a wordsmith who is able to see Yahweh in language and share that facet of Him with others. She has had a remarkable journey so far with Yahweh, overcoming depression and anxieties to discover the great joy that Yahweh has for her in this life. One of the ways Yahweh has helped her overcome so much is through writing. He also speaks to her through her poems. She is excited to share the unique facet of Him that she sees with you via this anthology and she hopes that you will realize the special Promise that Yahweh made to Himself through you as you read these poems. She has always found Yahweh to be faithful and she looks forward to where He is taking her next. She lives and teaches in Northwest Arkansas and has a spoiled Yorkie named Scrappy. She enjoys stories in all forms, including music, movies, and books. She also enjoys spending time with friends. She writes two blogs on Blogspot: Shine and Zadokim.